40

IN HIS PRESENCE

SERIES 2 and 3 EDITION

A prayer book and guide to
Confirmation, Communion
and Church Teaching

by

DENIS E. TAYLOR

lately Dean of B...

CW00684547

RELIGIOUS EDUCATION PRESS
A member of the Pergamon Group
Headington Hill Hall · Oxford

Printed in Great Britain by
A. Wheaton & Co, Exeter

ISBN 0 08 017186 9 flexicover   ISBN 0 08 017605 4 hard cover

FOREWORD

By the former Bishop of St. Andrews

A BOOK is like a child. After it is conceived in its author's mind it remains hidden and secret while it slowly takes shape, but on its appearance in the world it assumes an independent life of its own, its begetter looking on with wistful hope, trusting that it may find a welcome and have a prosperous life.

Next to the privilege of being a father is the honour of being a god-father; and I am proud to stand sponsor for this little book which is now in your hands. Without doubt it will keep the 'promises' which are involved in its appearance. It is on the greatest of all subjects, on which our immortal well-being depends, and will teach its readers (old as well as young) how to 'draw near'.

Perhaps the highest praise I can give to it is to say that it is a characteristic product of its author, and he is well qualified to write it. As he grows older (like Wordsworth's 'Happy Warrior') he keeps undimmed in his mind the experience of youth; and now, with the wisdom of the mature, can speak with understanding to the heart of the young.

LUMSDEN BARKWAY.

The author and publishers acknowledge with gratitude the permission granted to them by the Registrars of the Convocations of Canterbury and York to use copyright material of the Second and Third Series Liturgies in this book.

CONTENTS

IN HIS PRESENCE

PART I: PRAYER

EACH NEW DAY

'I am with you alway.'

At the beginning of a new day our aim is to offer to God all that lies ahead and to ask for his help and for the knowledge that he is with us, present beside us all the time. For he *is* always with us, though we, busy with the day's work and cares, may often forget him.

On the morning before the battle of Edgehill, the Cavalier, Sir Jacob Astley, prayed:

> Lord, I shall be very busy this day.
>   If I forget thee,
> Do not thou forget me.

At the start of the new day, then let us offer it to our Father, praying above all that we may have a clear sense of his presence.

> Closer is he than breathing and
>   nearer than hands and feet.

Kneel. Remember that our Lord is very near. Say reverently and thoughtfully:

In the Name of the Father, and of the Son, and of the Holy Ghost.

Thank God for the rest and safety of the night now past, for health and powers renewed. Offer to God the day that is beginning:

O Blessed Lord, I thank thee for rest and safety through the hours of night.
For this new day in which to serve thee,
For powers of mind and body new once more,
I worship and adore thy glorious Name.

Praise and adore God, using these verses from the Te Deum:

We praise thee, O God: we acknowledge thee to be the Lord.
All the earth doth worship thee: the Father everlasting....
Heaven and earth are full: of the Majesty of thy glory....
The Holy Church throughout all the world: doth acknowledge thee;
The Father: of an infinite Majesty;
Thine honourable, true: and only Son;
Also the Holy Ghost: the Comforter.
Thou art the everlasting Son: of the Father....
Day by day: we magnify thee;
And we worship thy name: ever world without end....

PRAYERS

Vouchsafe, O Lord: to keep us this day without sin.

O Lord, have mercy upon us: have mercy upon us.

O Lord, let thy mercy lighten upon us: as our trust is in thee.

O Lord, in thee have I trusted: let me never be confounded.

Ask for help in the coming day:

Most Holy Jesus, Friend and Master, who art ever near, keep me this day from sin in all I think and do and say.

Enable me to know that thou art by my side to give me strength when I am tempted, wisdom when I am puzzled or in doubt.

O Blessed Lord, I offer these hours to thee. Make me a blessing to others this day. Enable me to know that in doing my work I am doing thy will and that in serving others I am serving thee.

So may I be blessed of thee, my Master and my Friend.

Try to be up in time to do some of your work of Intercession. Turn to pages 20 to 26 for this.

Our Father....Amen.

May the Grace of our Lord Jesus Christ, and the Love of God, and the fellowship of the Holy Spirit, be with me in all I do this day and for evermore. Amen.

THE PARTS OF PRAYER

*Each night our private prayers should be modelled
like this*

ADORATION   First—love, adore and
praise God in whom we live and move,
and have our being. Praise him for his
noble acts, praise him for his excellent
greatness. Adore him for Jesus Christ.
Love him because he first loved us and
gave himself for us.

CONFESSION   A sense of all that God is
and all he does for us at once brings
home our own unworthiness, how often
we fail to live up even to our own ideals,
how poor our fight against temptation,
how weak our efforts to pray better,
how uncostly our work for others and
for our Lord. So we confess these our
sins to God, and ask forgiveness.

THANKSGIVING   The knowledge that when
we are truly sorry and really mean to
do better, we are forgiven, makes
thankfulness well up in our hearts, and
we set ourselves to remember our
many blessings— health, home, food,
work, friends, play, our Church, all the
joy of being alive—and we return
thanks to God our Father.

SUPPLICATION Having adored God, having confessed our sinfulness, having thanked him for all his goodness and loving-kindness, then and then only we ask for more blessings. We make our supplications first for the needs of others, for great causes, for friends and for enemies. These are our Intercessions. Afterwards we pray for ourselves—we tell God our hopes, our joys, our fears, our desires, our needs. These are our Petitions.

Such prayers are A-C-T-S indeed,

true ACTS of worship

Kneel. *Remember that our Lord is very near. Say reverently and thoughtfully:*

In the name of the Father, and of the Son, and of the Holy Ghost.

Be very still. Let the rush and hurry of the day die away as you kneel in silence in his presence. Think of the wonder and majesty of God the Creator of this universe, of earth and sea, of stars and illimitable space. Try to express your wonder and love.

Adoration

Blessed be thou, O Lord God, for ever and ever. Thine, O Lord, is the greatness and the power and the glory, and the victory, and the majesty: for all that is in the heaven and in the earth is thine; thine is the Kingdom, O Lord, and thou art exalted as head above all. Both riches and honour come of thee, and thou reignest over all....Now, therefore, our God, we thank thee, and praise thy glorious name.

I will magnify thee, O God my King: and I will praise thy Name for ever and ever.
Jesu, my Lord, I thee adore.
O make me love thee more and more.

(Often use other words of adoration. Some are given on page 16.)

PRAYERS

Confession

Think back over the day. What good have you left undone? Have you said or done anything wrong or mean? Sometimes use the questions for self-examination on page 67. Always do this before Communion. When you have thought back carefully over the day, tell God where you have failed.

I confess to God Almighty, the Father, the Son, and the Holy Ghost, and before the whole company of heaven, that I have sinned in thought, word and deed through my own grievous fault. And specially I have failed in these ways. . . . Wherefore I pray God to have mercy upon me, to forgive me my sins, and to bring me to everlasting life.

Sometimes you may like to express special penitence in the solemn words of the 51st Psalm.

Have mercy upon me, O God, after thy great goodness: according to the multitude of thy mercies do away mine offences.
Wash me throughly from my wickedness: and cleanse me from my sin.
For I acknowledge my faults: and my sin is ever before me.
Make me a clean heart, O God: and renew a right spirit within me.

Pray earnestly in your own words for forgiveness.

Thanksgiving

Not only does God forgive our sins when we repent, and for this we should thank him gladly, but our life is full of blessings—health, home, food, friends, are only a few, and greatest blessing of all—the friendship of our Lord Jesus Christ. These suggestions may remind you of blessings for which to thank God:

Health	*Work*	*Clothing*
Parents	*Home*	*Food*
My Church	*Friends, especially:*	
Good times, especially:	*Beauty in God's handiwork, e.g., country, garden, sea.*	
Help in temptation, especially:	*Beauty in man's handiwork, e.g., music, painting, books.*	

When you have considered, then thank God with all your heart:

Almighty and everlasting God, I praise and thank thee for all thy countless goodness and mercies towards me. Especially I bless thee for:

Help me to be truly thankful for these and all thy good gifts by giving myself to thy service and by walking before thee in holiness and righteousness all my days; through Jesus Christ our Lord, to whom with thee and the Holy Ghost be all honour and glory, world without end. Amen.

PRAYERS

Supplication

There are, of course, some special people and needs you will wish to pray for every night:

Father....................   Mother....................

Husband or Wife....................

Home, Special difficulties.........   needs...........

Brothers....................   Sisters....................

Special Friends....................

Relations....................

Anyone seriously ill or dying....................

One who has died....................

My own needs and hopes....................

Turn to your Intercession Notes for each day of the week, pages 20 to 26.

Sum up your Adoration, Confession, Thanksgiving and Supplication in our Lord's own words

Our Father ...

Into Thy hands, O Lord, I commend myself and all for whom I have prayed this night. Keep us in thy loving care and bless us all, I beseech thee, Lord Jesus. Amen.

ACTS OF ADORATION

'O praise ye the Lord.'

Here are some glorious words with which to offer God your praise.

Holy, holy, holy, Lord God of hosts, heaven and earth are full of thy glory. Glory be to thee, O Lord most High.

Glory be to the Father, and to the Son, and to the Holy Ghost; as it was in the beginning, is now, and ever shall be, world without end.

Blessed art thou, O Lord of our fathers: praised and exalted above all for ever.
Blessed art thou for the Name of thy Majesty: praised and exalted above all for ever.
Blessed art thou in the temple of thy holiness: praised and exalted above all for ever. . . .
Blessed art thou on the glorious throne of thy Kingdom: praised and exalted above all for ever.
Blessed art thou in the firmament of heaven: praised and exalted above all for ever.

Scottish Prayer Book 1929.

To God the Father who loved us and made us accepted in the Beloved; to God the Son who loved us and loosed us from our sins by his own blood; to God the Holy Ghost who sheddeth the love of

God abroad in our hearts; to the one true God be all love and all glory for time and for eternity.

Revised Prayer Book 1928.

O Lord our Governor, how excellent is thy name in all the world: thou that hast set thy glory above the heavens! ...

For I will consider thy heavens, even the works of thy fingers: the moon and the stars which thou hast ordained.

What is man, that thou art mindful of him: and the son of man, that thou visitest him?

Thou madest him lower than the angels: to crown him with glory and worship. ...

O Lord our Governor: how excellent is thy name in all the world!

Ps. viii.

Praise the Lord, O my soul: O Lord my God, thou art become exceeding glorious; thou art clothed with majesty and honour.

Thou deckest thyself with light as it were with a garment: and spreadest out the heavens like a curtain:

... Praise thou the Lord, O my soul, praise the Lord.

Ps. civ. 1-4.

Our hymnbooks contain many magnificent acts of praise. Use these sometimes in your private prayers, e.g.

Holy, holy, holy, Lord God Almighty

and

My God, how wonderful thou art.

A SCHEME OF INTERCESSION

To pray for others, that is, to intercede, is a most important work. It is real work, hard work, service of the highest order.

If we only pray for ourselves, and maybe, our little circle, our prayers are really selfish. How tired we get of folk who can only talk about themselves! We do not want God to feel like that 'about us.

There is service and adventure in learning to take your part in the prayer work of the Church. You will find it makes your prayers more interesting and satisfying. You *know* you have done something useful and important.

But it is not easy. There are many difficulties, such as wandering thoughts, and your own weariness at bedtime. Why not make it your habit to drop in to your church for ten minutes on your way home from work every day to do this other work? If you do not pass near enough for that, could you not make your prayer time immediately after your meal, before going out for the evening?

Above all perseverance is needed. The Devil will try hard to break down any good habit you build up— he will put many difficulties in the way.

Remember that Jesus told us to go on praying and not grow weary of trying. He reminded us that perseverance in prayer is rewarded when he told of the widow who cried to an unjust judge for justice day after day, until the man at last granted her request because he was so thoroughly sick of her! Imagine our Lord likening himself to an unjust judge! But there are several stories Jesus told with a twinkle in his eye. One of these was on this subject of persevering in intercession—about the man who needed bread for a belated traveller and went to knock up a neighbour, already in bed, to borrow a loaf. He went on shouting for it till the neighbour just *had* to get up and give it. We are to persevere with our prayers.

Prayer is work. Work needs method.

On the next pages there is a scheme for Intercession arranged over the days of the week. Without an ordered scheme you are bound to forget much for which you should be praying. Hence this scheme for each day of the week and space to add your own notes.

A PRAYER NOTE BOOK

SUNDAY— **The Church of God**

Sunday is the weekly commemoration of the rising of Christ from the tomb, to live and reign for evermore. The Church carries on his work.

Pray for

Your Bishop(s).   Your own parish clergy.

Members of your congregation, especially............

Church workers—Choir, Sunday School Teachers, Sidesmen, Servers, Wardens, Vestry, Ladies' Guild members, etc. Especially................................

More priests. Remember the need of more man-power at home and overseas. For any thinking of ordination...

The world-wide Church. Any need (e.g., unity, greater faith, converting the indifferent)..............

Any approaching great world event affecting the whole Church ....

That Christians may learn to give generously of their money and time in God's service.

That priests and lay people may strive to bring those outside who never worship into membership.

MONDAY — **The Church Overseas**

(Pause to remember that but for the missionary zeal of the Apostles and early Christians we should have been left in paganism and fear. A first duty of a Christian is to win others to Christ. Thank God for the heroism of missionaries and that in most lands today there is a strong indigenous Church.)

Pray for

Any Missionary you know personally.................

Mission priests, doctors, nurses, teachers, agriculturalists, carpenters and mechanics, especially
....

The people among whom they work . . . that they may have faith, courage to overcome opposition of family or neighbours in accepting Christ.

Indigenous priests, catechists, teachers, that they may give a fine witness among their own people.

The Missionary Societies' home headquarters.

Removal of colour barriers so that racial segregation and hatred may be overcome.

Church people to understand still better and care more for the world mission of the Church.

(If you know little about the great work overseas ask the clergy for the monthly papers published by all Missionary Societies.)

TUESDAY — **The Nations**

(Think of the events which are in the news, international problems, racial difficulties, peoples striving for independence, etc., etc.)

Bring to God the happenings which seem to you most urgent or dangerous and pray that God's will may be done.

Pray for

The United Nations that it may build true fellowship between the nations.

The hungry in many lands.

Our own statesmen, especially............................

Leaders of other lands, especially ....

The people in lands without political freedom
....

Any who lead in the struggle for freedom............

Christians persecuted for their religion or politics, or in fear or want, especially............................

Clubs and Fellowships

Pray for

Any Club, Association or Fellowship, youth or adult, to which you belong—sporting, trade unionist, political, cultural or religious.

Members, especially.....................................

Chaplain ....

Particular needs or problems............................

Pray for

Your office, shop or factory friends....................

The head, and others in authority....................

Those working in difficult, dangerous, or un-
healthy conditions.

*(If you do not know any personally, pray for
miners, seamen, iron workers at blast furnaces,
etc., those on night shift.)*

Any unemployed or in money difficulties............

Any unhappy in their jobs.............................

Anyone unpopular.......................................

Difficulties at work.....................................

Schools, Colleges and Universities

Pray for

Your School, College or University....................

Your friends, especially................................

Teachers, lecturers, that they may inspire a love
of the Christian Faith, and appreciation of beauty,
truth and real goodness................................

All keen young Church people to see in teaching a
great field of service for Christ........................

Any thinking of teaching, especially.................

THURSDAY—**The Lonely and Old**

Thursday is the day of Christ's lonely temptation in the Garden of Gethsemane.

Pray for

The lonely, especially old people who have no one to care for and love them.
Especially ....

Thursday was also the day of Christ's Ascension to Heaven.

Thank God for the triumph of Jesus.

The Nation and Commonwealth

Pray for

Any part of the Commonwealth you know............

Any Commonwealth problem (e.g., racial unity, political independence) ....

The Sovereign and Royal Family.......................

The Prime Minister ....

Any M.P., local councillor, or magistrate, especially
....

Urgent local or national questions (e.g., housing, crime, etc.)...

All the nations of the Commonwealth to be a power for peace throughout the world.

FRIDAY—**All Who Need Christ's Love**

Friday is the day of the Crucifixion of Jesus.

Pray for

A clearer realisation of God's great love for us— love so great that he was willing to die for us.

Greater willingness to work for God.

Unbelievers—any you know who seldom or never worship God, especially ....
(Perhaps someone in your office or home.)

Children without parents or home or religion, especially ....

Pray for

Doctors and Nurses, especially ....
(Think of them in consulting room and hospital. Remember by name any you know.)

Sufferers. Any ill or suffering person you know.
Lift them up to our Lord who loves them and suffered for all. Pray for each by name.

Old people, especially.....................................
Church Homes for aged, especially.......................
(If you do not know any Church Orphanages, Rescue Homes, Hostels, or Homes for old folk, ask your clergy to get someone along to talk about them. Much good work is little known. Much help is needed.)

Pray for

The Faithful departed, especially ....

SATURDAY— **The Church at Home**

Pray for

More manpower.

> *(Think of the inadequacy of one Priest to thousands of people. Pray that more men will feel the call to the Priesthood. They may not be conscious that God is calling them. Your prayers may help them realise.)*

Pray for

More women workers, as missionaries, nurses, teachers, youth leaders, community centre workers, deaconesses or Sunday-school teachers.

> *(Pray for any whom you think God might use in these ways. Perhaps he wants you?)*

Pray that

Churchpeople may rise to the challenge to bring the Church to new housing areas. For this work in your diocese.

Pray for

Any special project in your own Congregation
....
Sunday-schools ....
Efforts to reach young people who attend no Church ....
Any preparing for Confirmation, especially.........
....

> *(Are you making your Communion tomorrow? Turn to p. 59.)*

PART II: THE CHURCH

WHAT IS THE CHURCH?

What is the Church? A Society—a divine Society because founded by Jesus Christ. Whit-sunday is called the Birthday of the Church.

What is the Church for? To carry on what Jesus began—to teach people the goodness, holiness and love of God and his purpose for men; to restore the relationship between God and man broken by man's disobedience which we call sin. The Church is to be the family of God's people, uniting them in worship and in work to set up his reign of justice and love, and helping them to bear witness to him by the quality of their lives.

How do we become members? Entrance to Church is by Baptism, in which a person is made a member of Christ, the child of God and an inheritor of the Kingdom of Heaven.

What do members try to do? *Renounce*, that is, have nothing to do with anything evil, mean or second rate; *believe* and be tremendously happy about our Christian faith; *keep* God's holy will and commandments made plain through the Bible, the teaching of the Church, and our conscience; be fellow-workers with Jesus in spreading kindness and joy, setting up the reign of God on earth, his 'kingdom' of goodness and love; join together to worship and adore our Creator, the God 'Who made and loveth all.' Members try by prayer, the sacraments, self-discipline and service to grow in the knowledge and love of Jesus.

27

What does the Church do for her members? Calls
them together for worship; is the channel whereby
God strengthens them for the difficulties and tempta-
tions of life by giving them the Holy Spirit in Baptism
and Confirmation; refreshes them constantly through
the Sacrament of the Body and Blood of Christ.

Teaches them about God, his intentions for men
and their eternal destiny; gives them special help at
the cross-roads of life, e.g., marriage, illness; acts as
a channel whereby the repentant receive forgiveness
joins them in a happy fellowship, the Church, an
army pledged to carry on the work Christ began.

The Church includes not only her members in this
world, The Church Militant here on earth (militant
means fighting, i.e., waging war against sin and evil)
but also those who have passed on to the life beyond
They are called the Church Expectant (i.e., waiting
while being made perfect) and the Church Triumphant
in Heaven.

Who are the Church's Ministers? The Church has
a threefold ministry: Bishops, Priests and Deacons
A man is made deacon first, and may not celebrate
Holy Communion, pronounce Absolution nor give the
Blessing. After one year as deacon he is ordained
priest and can exercise every function of the Ministry
except those reserved for Bishops (following the
example of the Apostles).

Bishops only may administer Confirmation (see
Acts 8 quoted below) or ordain a man as deacon or
priest. The Bishops take the place of the Apostles
deriving their authority from Christ's commission to
the Apostles, handed down to them today. This is
called the Apostolic Succession. Bishops have over-
sight of dioceses. These may have as few as a dozen
parishes, but in some countries have as many as four
or five hundred. Titles vary from country to country

28

but the bishop of a large diocese may have a suffragan or assistant bishop(s) and also be aided by archdeacons and rural deans who supervise groups of parishes. The dean is the chief minister of the cathedral; but if the cathedral has a parish the title provost is used.

A group of dioceses forms a province under an Archbishop, who may be referred to as the Metropolitan. In Scotland the title Archbishop is avoided and the bishop elected head of the province is called the Primus, meaning 'first among equals'. Where a country has several provinces (e.g. Canada) one of the Archbishops is appointed Primate. In many countries dioceses and provinces work together through a General Synod; in England, through the Church Assembly and Convocations.

CONFIRMATION

Confirmation is in the Bible. It was practised by the Apostles. We read about it in the New Testament. The Church has administered it ever since.

Confirmation: in the New Testament
From Acts, Chap. 8

'Then Philip went down to Samaria and preached Christ unto them. . . . When they believed Philip preaching the things concerning the kingdom of God and the name of Jesus Christ, they were baptised, both men and women. . . . Now when the apostles which were at Jerusalem heard that Samaria had received the word of God, they sent unto them Peter and John: who, when they were come down, prayed for them, that they might receive the Holy Ghost. . . . Then laid they their hands on them, and they received the Holy Ghost.

Confirmation: receiving the Holy Spirit

Philip had gone to Samaria preaching and teaching. He baptised his converts, just as your priest would. Then the Apostles came from Jerusalem and 'laid their hands on them and they received the Holy Ghost, i.e., confirmed them. In the same way after you have been carefully instructed and prepared, the Bishop comes and 'lays his hands' upon you, and you *receive the Holy Ghost*. The word 'confirmation,' a convenient name for this, came later. The word means 'strengthening'.

Confirmation: the promises

At your Baptism (if in infancy) Godparents made promises on your behalf. At Confirmation you make these promises yourself. You shoulder the responsibility because you are now a responsible person. But it is one thing to make a promise—it is quite another to keep that promise. You need special help, God's help. The Church calls it 'grace', strength greater than your own, power from the Holy Spirit. That power is given you at Confirmation, the laying on of hands being the outward visible sign. But it is neither automatic nor magic. You must call on that power and use it. It's rather like a cheque—little good to you till you cash it. Just having it in your pocket won't keep you from hunger.

When you are conFIRMed you make firm those promises, and are made firm to keep them by the grace and strength given you.

Confirmation: strength for living

Think of Confirmation as your special ordination or equipping with strength by God for your life's work. As the Sovereign when anointed at coronation is given grace to rule, or a Bishop at his consecration is given grace for his high office, so you at Confirmation are given grace for your life's work, which is to fight under Christ's banner against sin, the world and the devil and to continue Christ's faithful soldier and servant unto your life's end.

Confirmation: a beginning

In this way Confirmation continues the process begun at Baptism. But it must not end it. That strength of the Holy Spirit given at Confirmation must be fed regularly all through your life by the Holy Communion.

THE DUTIES OF A CHURCHMAN

A Christian must live a life of discipline. Certain things are *duties*—a word not liked nowadays. They must be done always—whether we feel in the mood or not. It is by drilling ourselves to do these things that the strength of character necessary for resisting temptation is won. But we cannot do this alone in our own strength. We can do it only with God's help. The secret is to remember our Lord's presence, the power of his Holy Spirit, 'the One who stands by to help.' This power has been given to us and we must learn to call on and trust him whose strength is sufficient for us. Because a Christian knows he is never alone and practises the presence of Christ, he will be a happy, cheerful person, never downcast for long. He will be kind in his remarks and judgments about other people, always looking for the best in others. In Jesus' company (and we are in his company) we should be ashamed to say or think a mean thing, nor should we grumble or be gloomy.

So the duties of a Churchman, which help us to know Christ's presence, lead us to inward peace, quietness, and joy. We shall have the royalty of inward happiness.

These are the duties of a Churchman:

DUTY TO GOD

Worship

This is the foundation on which all else is built. By Jesus' own example in attending his place of worship, the synagogue, week by week, and also because we are told plainly in the Bible, we know that worship is the first duty of a Christian.

'Worship' means 'making God of most worth.'

The Holy Communion is the most important act of the Church's worship. Every Churchman should put it first in obedience to our Lord's command, 'DO THIS in remembrance of me.' He should return to one other service to hear instruction and to give thanks for his Communion.

Prayer

Our Lord often rose a great while before the day to have enough time in his busy life for prayer. A Christian should always begin the day with prayer, and be in touch with his Heavenly Father again before he goes to bed at night. He will practise the presence of Christ, that is, remember that our Lord is with him all the time; and he will often send little 'arrow prayers'—messages of thanks, or love, or calls for help—winging their way to him.

Bible Reading

Daily reading of the Bible is far more important to a Christian than reading the daily papers. The Bible is the Christian's daily *good* news. It is one of the vital links between God and man. Read carefully about this on page 37.

H.P.—B

Self-Discipline

'The good I would I do not and the evil that I would not that I do,' said St. Paul. Even he had a fight to rule himself. 'Every man that striveth for mastery is temperate (i.e., disciplined) in all things. They do it to obtain a corruptible crown, but we an incorruptible. I therefore . . . keep under my body and bring it into subjection.'

Mastery over self is only won by constant self-discipline, and the greatest help to this is the keeping of our rule of life, that is the rules we make for ourselves about our prayers, worship, communion, reading of the Bible, etc.

'Fasting' is a useful aid towards this self-discipline. It means self-control in our eating, learning to deny ourselves certain foods. For example, it has for long been a custom of the Church to abstain from eating meat on Friday, the day of our Lord's crucifixion, and on the main fast days of the Christian Year, that we may be reminded of his sacrifice for us. He did so much for us. We can surely do a little thing like that in acknowledgment.

Almsgiving

None of our possessions are *really* ours. God allows us the use of them. We are only stewards. This is particularly true of our money. We must put it to the best and most unselfish use.

(a) We must decide how much we ought to give to the upkeep of our church. A regular payment system like the stewardship envelope is much better than the haphazard coin in the plate. But supporting our Church is not *giving*. It is only *paying* for what we need, just as we pay for food or clothing. It is a debt of honour, because no bill is sent.

(b) Mission is a direct command of Jesus: 'Go ye, teach all nations and baptise them.' Many can only obey by giving and by prayer.

(c) Good causes make a claim on Christian generosity. Fighting hunger and disease in many lands; care of the aged, sick or homeless; helping young and old through clubs, etc., etc.

DUTY TO OUR NEIGHBOUR

Service

We are stewards not only of our money but also of our abilities and of our time. These must be used, not only for our own enjoyment, but for the good of others. So a Christian seeks ways in which to serve. The method matters little so long as we are giving of ourself for the benefit of others. One may teach in a Sunday-school, another may run a Guide Company, a third may sit at home to release a parent to get out for a little relaxation. We give invaluable service by being dependable and regular in any organisation to which we belong. There are also civic and social duties, vital fields of service, neglect of which has weakened the Church.

These duties are summed up in this

Short Guide to the
Duties of Church Membership

*Authorised by the
Archbishops of Canterbury and York*

All baptised and confirmed members of the Church must play their full part in its life and witness. That you may fulfil this duty we call upon you:

To follow the example of Christ in home and daily life, and to bear personal witness to him.

To be regular in private prayer day by day.

To read the Bible carefully.

To come to Church every Sunday.

To receive the Holy Communion faithfully and regularly.

To give personal service to Church, neighbours and community.

To give money for the work of the parish and diocese and for the work of the Church at home and overseas.

To uphold the standard of marriage entrusted by Christ to his Church.

To care that children are brought up to love and serve the Lord.

THE CHURCH'S BOOKS

I. THE BIBLE

'The most valuable thing this world affords,' is
how the Archbishop of Canterbury describes the
Bible when, at the Coronation of our Sovereigns in
Westminster Abbey, he hands the Holy Scriptures to
the Monarch. Yet an American journalist could give
the title 'The Book Nobody Knows' to a book he wrote
about the Bible. The most valuable thing this world
affords—the book nobody knows. Can this be so?
Certainly few today know it as well as earlier genera-
tions and the whole nation is thereby poorer.

Why is the Bible so Valuable?

(1) Because it is the record, divinely inspired, of
God's dealings with mankind. The Old Testament
traces the ways in which God revealed his nature to
men and women, and tried to make them understand
his laws, what he required from them, and his love
for rich and poor alike.

The Old Testament shows how the way was prepared over the centuries for the coming into the world
of Jesus Christ.

The New Testament contains four lives of Jesus
(the Gospels), or more correctly, accounts of his
ministry; a history of the earliest days of the Church
(the Acts of the Apostles); and letters from the
Apostles to congregations they had established, or to
men and women who had been their friends in this
work (the Epistles.)

(2) Because the study of the Bible—the reading of a
passage, imagining it all, and then thinking over

carefully what it means for us today—is one of God's appointed ways of speaking in our hearts, and making his will known.

Why 'The Book Nobody Knows'?

The Bible is not simply a book, but rather a library, for there are sixty-six books (not counting the section called the Apocrypha). The oldest books in the Old Testament were written seven or eight hundred years B.C. (before the birth of Christ); the New Testament all in the 1st century A.D. (Anno Domini, in the year of our Lord, i.e., since the Birth of Christ). People so long ago had different ways of thought and fashions of speech. They would have been as puzzled by our ways as we today find theirs difficult and misleading.

Then, too, the books of the Bible have been translated out of their original Hebrew or other ancient tongues.

The translation mostly used in church, the 'Authorised Version', was made over 300 years ago at the command of James I. Words develop rather different meanings over such a long period. Clearly we need all the help we can get if we are to have the greatest benefit from this 'most valuable thing the world affords.'

New translations in up-to-date English are in great demand today. You should get one of these. Perhaps they are of most help in the Epistles. St. Paul dictated his letters. He got far too engrossed to think of pausing for a full-stop and quite forgot to keep his sentences short. The new translations correct this and make the Epistles vivid and understandable.

How to Read the Bible

How much of the Bible you read is not nearly so important as *how you read it*. Offer a prayer first that God may speak to you through the passage chosen. Then read very slowly, making a great effort of imagination. Picture the scene, 'get inside' what you are reading, feel yourself there and taking part. Try to apply it to yourself. What is the message for you? Probably you will want to say a prayer about it.

All this is an art—it needs practice. Don't be disappointed if you do not get on too well at first. Persevere.

Join the Bible Reading Fellowship

For a trifling sum you receive a pamphlet setting a few verses for each day. An explanation of the passage is given—just a paragraph—and a suggestion of how it applies to your own life. The Bible Reading Fellowship gives you just the help you need and which it is difficult to do without. Ask your Priest about it. He will strongly approve. It is used all round the world. The address of the B.R.F. is 12 Buckingham Palace Gardens, London, S.W.1.

THE CHURCH'S BOOKS

II. THE PRAYER BOOK

Many parts of the Anglican Communion throughout the world today have their own Prayer Book, but all are descended from a common ancestor, the English Book of Common Prayer.

It was in the fifteen hundreds that the Church's services were first held in English. Till then they had been in Latin. Archbishop Cranmer was the great artist in words to whom we owe much of the stately English of the Book of Common Prayer.

The monks had seven 'Hours' of prayer—services or 'offices', said or sung every day. Out of these Cranmer constructed Mattins and Evensong. He divided the Psalms into the thirty morning and evening sections as we know them. The Latin titles which still remain remind us that services were once all in that language.

Another of the old 'Hours' is Compline. This lovely bedtime service, although dropped from the Book of Common Prayer in England, has found its way back into Anglican Prayer Books around the world, for example the Scottish and Canadian. (It is appended to the 1928 Book.)

The Holy Communion is everywhere the heart of the Church's worship. Many countries have restored ancient features discarded by the reformers in England. Thus Scotland, Canada and other countries have their own Liturgies. These bear a strong family resemblance and are clearly descended from a common source.

The Prayer Book contains the special prayers 'collects', and readings from the Epistles and the Gospels for every Sunday and Holy Day of the

Christian Year. When you cannot be at Church on a Holy Day make a practice of reading at home the Collect, Epistle and Gospel appointed.

The Prayer Book also has other great offices for our well-being: Baptism, when we enter the Church; the Catechism, an instruction in the Christian Faith; Confirmation, when we are strengthened for our life's work; Holy Matrimony, when God gives men and women grace to live in a special union which should be holy; the Visitation of the Sick, for help in times of bodily weakness; the Burial service, when the Church lays to rest our discarded bodies.

The Ordinal contains the forms of service when men are ordained for the Ministry, as deacons, priests or bishops.

This wonderful treasury also contains the Psalms, the hymnbook of the Jews, which Jesus often quoted and must have known by heart.

The Prayer Book is a precious heritage, be it the English Book revised in 1662, or the attempted revision of 1928; the revised Scottish Book of 1929, the new Canadian Book of 1962; or their first cousins of U.S.A., South Africa, and other parts of the Anglican Communion.

Use the Prayer Book for what it is—the Book of Common Prayer, which means the Book of Prayer for everyone.

THE CHURCH'S YEAR

The Church Calendar begins with

ADVENT SUNDAY

(either the last Sunday in November or the first in December).

There are four Sundays in Advent and during this period the Church prepares for

CHRISTMAS

the celebration of the Birthday or First Coming of Jesus when he was born at Bethlehem, and the Son of God became man.

EPIPHANY

commemorates the revealing ('showing forth' is the exact meaning of the word) of the Divine Nature, first to the Wise Men from the East. It is observed on January 6th. There are two to six Sundays after Epiphany. Then Septuagesima, Sexagesima, and Quinquagesima Sundays give warning of

ASH WEDNESDAY

(preceded by Shrove Tuesday, when people confessed their sins), which is the first day of

LENT

This solemn period of discipline, repentance and growth lasts roughly forty days, the period of our Lord's special preparation in the wilderness for the opening of his Ministry. The fourth Sunday in Lent is often kept as Mothering Sunday. The fifth Sunday in Lent is called Passion Sunday. Next comes Palm Sunday, when Jesus entered into Jerusalem for the final week of teaching in the Temple, known as

HOLY WEEK

which led up to the Last Supper, on Maundy Thursday evening, immediately before he went to the Garden of Gethsemane. There he was betrayed, and taken away for trial before the High Priest in the early morning and afterwards condemned by Pontius Pilate, the Roman Governor. He was crucified later that day, called

GOOD FRIDAY

He rose from the grave on the first day of the week,

EASTER DAY

and of this event every Sunday is the commemoration week by week.

There follow the great Forty Days, when Christ appeared frequently to the disciples and others, teaching and preparing them. He withdrew his bodily presence on

ASCENSION DAY

which, being the fortieth day after Easter, always falls on a Thursday. As Christ had promised, after ten days of waiting and prayer in the Upper Room in Jerusalem, the disciples received the Holy Spirit on

43

WHITSUNDAY

The Holy Spirit was to lead them into all truth and strengthen them for the colossal task of making Christ known to the uttermost parts of the earth, to all men, everywhere, in all ages. Whitsunday, also called Pentecost, is often known as the birthday of the Church. As the day of the original bestowing of the Holy Spirit, it was a favourite day for Baptism. A week later, on

TRINITY SUNDAY

the Church acknowledges the glory of the Eternal Trinity, Father, Son and Holy Spirit; and for the remaining twenty-five Sundays of the year, considers the great teachings and lessons of the faith once delivered. In these the Holy Spirit is ever leading us to perceive new depths of meaning, new relevancy for the changes and chances of the passing years and the developing social scene.

At the beginning of the Prayer Book is a Calendar showing the dates when the Church honours her heroes. The Apostles are each commemorated and also some of the greatest of the Saints, and all are remembered together on All Saints' Day. The Blessed Virgin Mary is honoured on several days, especially the Purification or Candlemas (February 2nd), and the Annunciation or Lady Day (March 25th).

On Michaelmas the Church reverences those higher ranks of God's creation, the Holy Angels.

THE CHURCH'S COLOURS

Each type of Festival and Fast has its distinctive colour—shown in Altar frontal, vestments, stole, pulpit fall and book markers. The colours thus announce the Church's Year.

These are the main colours and their meaning:

WHITE (or Cream or Gold): The joyful Festivals, especially Christmas, Easter and Ascension. Also for saints other than martyrs.

RED is the colour of fire and blood, so is used for Whitsunday and for martyrs.

PURPLE speaks of penitence and preparation—so is used in Lent and Advent.

GREEN, the ordinary colour of nature, suggests God's provision for our needs—so green is for ordinary, non-festival Sundays.

THE CHURCH'S CLOTHES
—THE VESTMENTS

Distinctive dress for various functions is worn in many callings. Not many have as long a history as Church vestments, which are adaptations of the classical costumes of the Roman Empire. As styles went out of fashion for everyday wear they were retained in Church use, and with modification have come down to us today. In the illustrations you will see the main vestments, and below is a list of their names and uses.

ALB —long white linen garment reaching to the ankles, derived from ancient tunic.

AMICE —once a neckcloth, has now become a linen square worn round the neck to protect the other vestments. Often decorated with an apparel.

APPARELS —ornamental panels at the foot of the alb, front and back, and on amice.

CASSOCK —the long black gown worn under other vestments. It used to be the day-to-day working costume of the clergy, not merely used in church. Some are again wearing it for day-to-day use. A bishop's cassock is purple, symbolical of rank.

CHASUBLE —worn by priest or bishop when celebrating the Holy Communion. It is descended from the commonest outdoor garment of classical times.

CHIMERE —of black or scarlet, open in front, worn by bishops over the rochet.

COPE —in the pre-Christian era it was a long cloak. It has become a costly embroidered vestment worn by bishops on occasions such as Confirmations or Ordinations, and by priests in Processions on Festivals, etc.

COTTA —similar to surplice, but shorter especially in the sleeves. Sometimes used by clergy and servers in place of surplice.

a Surplice
b Scarf
c Cassock
d Hood

47

A Amice	E Girdle	I Veil	M Purificator
B Stole	F Alb	J Maniple	N Chalice
C Chasuble	G Apparel	K Burse	O Corporal
D Orphrey	H Burse	L Pall	P Paten

A Hood
B Chimere
C Scarf   D Rochet   E Cassock

49

A MITRE

B EPISCOPAL RING

C PECTORAL CROSS

D STOLE

E GIRDLE

F ALB

G COPE

H APPAREL

I CROZIER OR PASTORAL STAFF

GIRDLE —a cord used to secure the alb or cassock round the waist.

HOOD —worn by clergy at choir offices (Mattins and Evensong, etc.). Was a mediaeval headdress, as name implies, but now worn hanging down the back. It denotes a university degree. Each has its distinctive colour.

MANIPLE —originally a napkin. It is worn over the left arm by bishops, priests and deacons at the Eucharist. It probably came into Church use to cleanse the vessels after the stole had developed as described below.

MITRE —the head-dress of a bishop. Mitres are tongue-shaped and remind us of the tongues of fire which lighted on the Apostles at Pentecost.

ORPHREYS —the embroidered strips, usually cross-shaped, on a chasuble.

ROCHET —worn by bishops. It is like an alb, but is used without girdle or apparels.

STOLE —was once a napkin or towel carried by ser-vants on the left shoulder. It became folded and narrow. As the deacons' duty was to cleanse the sacred vessels they wear it over the left shoulder. Priests wear the stole over both shoulders. The stole is worn at all the sacraments.

SURPLICE —of white linen, reaching to the knees. Is worn by choir and servers as well as clergy.

TIPPET —the black scarf worn with the hood at the choir offices, etc.

PART III:

THE HOLY COMMUNION

WHAT IS
THE HOLY COMMUNION?

On the night Jesus was betrayed to his enemies and taken to be crucified, at the last supper with his friends in that upper room in Jerusalem, he gave thanks and brake bread which he blessed and they all shared, and he said: 'This is my Body which is given for you. Do this in remembrance of me.' And he blessed wine and said: 'Drink ye all of this, for this is my Blood of the New Testament, which is shed for you and for many for the remission of sins: Do this, as oft as ye shall drink it, in remembrance of me.'

The Jews were used to a ceremonial meal as part of their worship of God, and Jesus at the Last Supper gave his friends a direct command which they could appreciate and obey. From that day to this the Sacrament of the Lord's Supper has been the central act of worship of the Church. It is known by at least six names: The Lord's Supper, The Holy Communion, The Holy Eucharist, The Blessed Sacrament (of the Body and Blood of Christ), The Mass, The Liturgy.

The Holy Communion is a Sacrament, the 'outward and visible sign of an inward and spiritual grace given unto us' in this way. The outward and visible sign is the Bread and Wine, blessed with the very words Jesus himself spake in the upper room. The inward and spiritual Grace given us is the divine life of Christ himself, grace, a share in the very nature of God. We are united with Christ, and his Spirit and Nature flow into us.

There are two parts of the Holy Communion: What man does, What God does.

What man does

The Holy Communion is a sacrifice, that is, a gift which people offer to God through their appointed priest, as a sign of their dependence on God, and in acknowledgment of God's absolute power and authority over them. 'Here we offer and present unto thee, O Lord, ourselves, our souls and bodies—to be a reasonable, holy and lively sacrifice unto thee.'

But we dare not offer anything so marred and sinful as we are except 'through Jesus Christ,' that is by joining our unworthy offering to his perfect offering of himself, spotless and sinless.

What God does

God accepts the offering of our sinful and unworthy selves because we unite our self-offering with the perfect offering of Jesus on Calvary. He gives to us through the Bread and Wine the divine life of Jesus, his 'grace and heavenly benediction.' He assures us of our membership with all the rest of the Church, both that part of it kneeling with us at those altar rails and other parts everywhere throughout the earth, as well as those departed from this world and now in the life beyond. We are privileged to be 'very members incorporate in the mystical body' of his Son, the Church, 'which is the blessed company of all faithful people.'

53

In the Holy Communion, everything in human life —our work, our homes, our love, our pleasure, leisure, hopes, fears, griefs, joys, our studies, ideas, successes, our sacrifices—all can be offered to God through Christ. All are represented in the Bread and Wine. God takes them up and consecrates them and gives them back together with the gift of divine life, so that in these things of daily life we can glorify and serve him.

Here is how a modern Prayer Book Catechism (the Canadian) puts it:

Question: Why was the Sacrament of the Lord's Supper ordained?

Answer: For the continual remembrance of the sacrifice of the death of Christ, and of the benefits which we receive thereby.

Question: What is the outward part or sign of the Lord's Supper?

Answer: Bread and Wine, which the Lord hath commanded to be received.

Question: What is the inward part, or thing signified?

Answer: The Body and Blood of Christ, which are verily and indeed taken and received by the faithful in the Lord's Supper.

Question: What benefits do we receive thereby?

Answer: The strengthening and refreshing of our souls and bodies unto eternal life by the Body and Blood of Christ.

HOW TO GO TO
THE HOLY COMMUNION

There are three reverent customs.

If you are going to receive Holy Communion:

Go early; go fasting; go well prepared.

Early. To receive Holy Communion is a most solemn thing. Put first things first. It has been the custom of the Church since the days of the Apostles to celebrate Holy Communion first thing in the morning, while the mind and body are fresh.

This is linked with the second rule, which is to go

Fasting. When possible, for reverence sake, and as an act of discipline, the Holy Food should be the first that passes your lips that day. That you may receive fasting according to the ancient custom of the Church is another reason for not receiving at a late Choral Eucharist, meant to be a great thanksgiving. Old or sick folk, or those who come from a distance, can only keep this rule in spirit and not in the letter. Try hard to keep this ancient custom. You will come to appreciate it. If for health reasons or other cause you have to break it, consult your priest and ask his approval.

Well prepared. This is vitally important. It is dealt with fully on page 59.

WHY HOLY COMMUNION IS
SOMETIMES 'SAID,'
SOMETIMES 'SUNG'

Most churches have Holy Communion early, perhaps at 7 or 8 a.m., perhaps at 9.30 a.m. The earlier service is almost sure to be 'said,' quite simply with no singing or sermon. Many churches today have a 'Family' or 'Parish' Communion at about 9 a.m., usually with simple singing and a short sermon, and often with a breakfast afterwards in the Church Hall.

This is excellent because the meal together expresses the fellowship which should exist among fellow-worshippers symbolised in the way all kneel together in fellowship at the Altar rails.

Both these services (and a similar 'said' celebration at about 12.30 p.m. after Mattins, meant for elderly people) are designed for people to 'make their Communion,' that is, to go to the Altar rails and receive the Blessed Sacrament.

Many churches have a choral celebration of the Holy Communion or Sung Eucharist at 11 a.m., when the Liturgy is sung, and there are hymns and a sermon. 'Eucharist' means 'The Great Thanksgiving.' That is the emphasis of this service. It is an act of thanksgiving and praise. Many may have received the Sacrament earlier that morning and have returned for this joyful thanksgiving.

It is important to remember that the Holy Communion, whether 'said' early or 'sung' late, is always the highest worship. There is no better place than that great Sacrament in which to worship our Lord present there among his people in such a special way.

OUR PREPARATION FOR
HOLY COMMUNION

The essential things are

TO KNOW PRECISELY

what you are going to

GIVE THANKS FOR

CONFESS

PRAY FOR

Vagueness is the curse of religion. The road to hell is paved with good intentions, the things we vaguely meant to do—but of course didn't. So be very definite and clear-cut.

Think out the night before your Communion, or earlier, just exactly what you will thank God for, what you must confess, the subject for which chiefly you will pray, pleading with God for this special and particular thing, or person, the sacrifice of Jesus on the Cross. This chief subject of our praying is known as our SPECIAL INTENTION

Go to Holy Communion so prepared that, were anyone suddenly to ask you as you entered the doors of the church, 'What are you going to THANK God for this morning?' without a moment's hesitation you could answer. In the same way, supposing you were suddenly asked 'What are you going to CONFESS to God this morning?' you could reply instantly. Or, again, if you were asked 'What is your INTENTION this morning?'—that is to say, 'For what, or for whom, are you going to PRAY chiefly?' at once you could give a definite answer.

That is the essence of a good preparation.

St. Paul said:

'Whosoever shall eat this bread and drink this cup of the Lord unworthily, shall be guilty of the body and blood of the Lord. But let a man examine himself, and so let him eat that bread and drink of that cup.'

To help you to know what you ought to confess, use the questions on page 67 to examine yourself.

THE SILENCES AT
HOLY COMMUNION

The 'Early Service', when Holy Communion is *said* (in contrast to *sung*), differs from other services in having long silences. On the right use of these silences depends whether you come away feeling you have really prayed and worshipped, or instead come away knowing that your thoughts wandered, and you did not really concentrate on your praying. How vexed you feel! Much depends on the right use of those silences. Try this plan:—

Before the Service Begins

People usually kneel all the time until the Holy Communion service begins. In this silence go over in your mind your preparation. Lay out ready, as it were, those things you decided to *thank* God for, to *confess*, and to *pray* for. Consider each carefully. Offer each to our Lord. Pray about them. When the priest enters

60

and goes to the Altar there is still a minute of silence left, so pray for him and the server too, if there is one. Pray for your fellow communicants in the church.

During the Offertory

The second silence comes after the Creed at the Offertory. It is the time for the *thanksgivings* of your preparation. The Bread and Wine are being placed on the Altar. Simultaneously the offerings of the congregation are being taken. The Bread and Wine are things people have made. They represent our work, our whole life. They are going to be offered to God. Offer your own work, all you do all day long, to God. Then *thank* him. The money you have put in the plate is your acknowledgment that all you have depends on him. He can let you have it, or take it away. Offer him your thanksgivings for all you have and are.

At the Communion

The third silence is just before the people go to the Altar to receive the consecrated Bread and Wine. In this silence *adore* him. Try to realise that he is there with you in the church, his house. Though unseen and invisible he is just as truly present. You cannot see the air, but you breathe it. This Communion is a meeting place with your Lord. Kneel, yes, and tremble before him.

> Thee we adore, O hidden Saviour, thee,
> Who in thy Sacrament dost deign to be;
> Both Flesh and Spirit at thy Presence fail,
> Yet here thy Presence we devoutly hail.

Pour out your love, your worship. Now is the time to pray about your special intention, the people or matters you made ready at your preparation for this moment.

You go and kneel at the Altar rails. Worship and adore your Saviour. Bring Him again all that you decided in your preparation—your thanksgivings, confession, and special intercessions.

In the silence while the other people are making their Communion, continue to pray about these matters and tell him all that is in your heart. This silence is all too short.

After the Communion

The last silence is while the priest cleanses the Paten and Chalice. Use this silence to give thanks for the wonderful thing that has happened to you, for the precious gift of grace you have been given—that you have been with our Lord. From your confession there will likely arise a good resolution, e.g., if you have confessed neglect of your prayers, you must resolve most firmly to overcome this sin, and become faithful and regular in your praying. Make your resolution quite definite. It is the best possible way to thank our Lord.

Please read this chapter many times. Make sure you know by heart what to do in each silence. It is so important. Here is a summary:

Before the service begins: Go over your preparation. Lay out ready what you will thank for, confess, pray for. Pray for the priest.

At the Offertory: Thanksgiving. Offer your daily life and work.

At the Communion: Worship. Your intention.

After the Blessing: Thanksgivings. Good resolution.

Use this method Sunday by Sunday until it is your habit. It will help greatly.

PART IV:

THE FORGIVENESS OF SINS

HOW WE ARE FORGIVEN

Can you remember as a child getting into some scrape, and before you were forgiven having to go and tell your father you were sorry? It is the same in our religion. Before God forgives us our sins we must tell him we are sorry—we have to confess our sins. There are several things involved in this. First we must be truly sorry about our sins (and remember, the good we have failed to do, the prayers we have failed to offer, rank as sin just as much as the wrong or evil we have said or thought or done). It is more a matter of the *will* than of feelings, purposing with all the strength of character that we have, to improve—to do the good we have previously failed to do, to avoid the evil. But we must ask and use God's help, because we cannot do it in our own strength. Having that intention we tell God how we have failed. He knows already, of course, but like every father he wants us to own up, and *face* up. Jesus taught us that then, when we have done this, God removes the guilt. We are forgiven.

There are two ways of confessing our sins. Both bring forgiveness when we really repent, really intend to do better.

The first way is privately—it may be either kneeling by our own bedside or it may be in church—telling God in our own words in secret, what our sins have been, how firmly we mean to do better, and begging for forgiveness. When that is sincere God forgives. There is no doubt of that. We have Jesus' promise.

There are words to help in this in Evening Prayers on page 12.

The second way to confess our sins is to God in the presence of some 'discreet and learned minister of God's Word,' who will give us advice and help 'to the quietening of our conscience and the avoidance of all scruple and doubtfulness,' and then, acting as God's spokesman, assure us of God's forgiveness.

For more about this second way, see page 70.

Before using either we need to try to see ourselves as we must appear in God's sight. We take a rosy view of ourselves, and excuse ourselves too easily. We should, therefore, in self-examination, prod memory and conscience by questions designed to let us see ourselves more as God sees us and as we really are.

See below: Overhauling Ourselves; and page 66, Questions for Self-Examination.

OVERHAULING OURSELVES

Each evening in our prayers we review what we have done or left undone in the day now past, and ask forgiveness for the sins revealed.

Before each Communion (be it weekly, fortnightly, or monthly, or on special holy days of the Church, or on our birthday), we require to examine ourselves more strictly—else we shall not know precisely what we must confess. And unless we know what we are asking forgiveness for, how can we expect God to forgive us? For we must come cleansed and forgiven to our Communion. This forgiveness is the 'wedding garment' Christ told us we must wear at the King's banquet. So questions for Self-Examination are provided on this page, and the instruction on Forgiveness, page 64.

Just as houses require spring-cleaning, so we need 'spring-cleaning,' at least once a year, or probably more often. Before our Communion at the great Festivals, specially Easter and Christmas, is the best time for extra special overhaul, to see whether we are advancing or falling back in our fight to become people on whom Christ can rely.

For this, use with care the questions which follow, especially if you have decided to seek 'comfort and counsel' from some 'discreet and learned minister of God's Word,' as the Prayer Book puts it, in order to receive the 'benefit of absolution.'

Many who are trying hard to advance in service of our Lord and his Church have decided to do this if only for the spiritual counsel and advice received.

QUESTIONS FOR SELF-EXAMINATION

A good plan is to have paper and pencil and jot down the things we must confess. Just write single words, e.g. 'lying', 'jealousy', 'prayers missed'. You can put this paper in your Prayer Book and use it after you arrive in Church in the minutes before the service begins, praying about these sins and asking strength to overcome them. Having a paper ensures that you remember everything.

Kneel down. Think of our Lord on the Cross. Remember it was the wickedness and unlovingness of ordinary people like us which caused his death. Say a prayer such as this:

O Holy Spirit, help me now to know the truth about myself. Stir up my conscience and memory that I may perceive how I have failed. Show me my sins against God and my sins against my fellows, the evil I have done and the good I have left undone, that I may truly repent and determine to do better and overcome my faults, with thy help; for Jesus' sake.

The Things Left Undone

(Sins of Omission)

Have I omitted my morning prayers?—my evening prayers?—been careless in them?

Have I kept Sunday holy?

Have I stayed away from the Holy Communion on Sunday when I could have been there?

Have I prepared carefully before receiving Holy Communion?

Have I kept my rule about Bible reading?

Have I done what I ought and could—for the Church? —in my home?—for others?

Have I let slide a chance to do a kind act?—or say a kind word?—or stand up for my Faith?

Have I given as much money as I could afford for the work of the Church at home and overseas?

Have I really tried constantly to make God of most worth in my life?—or let dancing, the cinema, television, or lying in bed interfere with my duty to him?

The Things We Ought Not to Have Done

(Sins of Commission)

In Thought

Have I thought uncharitably about others?—been jealous?

Have I been conceited?—vain?—cocksure?—contemptuous?

Have I harboured malice or hatred in my heart?

Have I been spiteful?—unforgiving?

Have I let linger in my mind impure thoughts or imaginings, or desires?

In Word

Have I made fun of holy things?—spoken irreverently?—used God's name lightly?

Have I used bad language?—told dirty jokes?

Have I been strictly truthful?

Have I gossiped?—slandered others?—spoken unkindly about others?—boasted?

In Deed

Have I done my best at my work?

Have I stolen?—cheated?—delayed to pay my debts? —broken my word?

Have I been bad-tempered? — grumbled? — quarrelled?

Have I been greedy?—eaten or drunk more than my share or more than I needed?

Have I treated women and girls honourably, chivalrously and politely?—or tried to be smart?—to show off?

Have I made boys respect me?—or have I lowered the dignity of womanhood?

Have I been pure and clean and healthy in all that I do alone?—with others?

Have I taught evil to another?—set a bad example?— at home?—at work?—with my friends?

CONFESSION

To reach even a low standard of Christian living means a hard struggle. We are conscious of besetting sins which get the better of us constantly. We long for help in overcoming them. We know that our Lord is calling us not to a minimum standard but to holiness. How are we to attain it? Sometimes, too, old sins worry us. We do not feel 'right' with God.

The Prayer Book puts it this way: 'If there be any of you who by this means (i.e., private confession) cannot quiet his own conscience herein, but requireth further comfort or counsel, let him come to me or to some other discreet and learned minister of God's Word, and open his grief; that by the ministry of God's Holy Word he may receive the benefit of absolution, together with spiritual counsel and advice . . .'

The Church makes available to us skilled advice to help us in life's battle. Just as ailments of the body show symptoms which a doctor is trained to recognise and treat, so a priest who is a good director is trained to recognise the ailments of the soul and treat them through the 'spiritual counsel and advice' he gives.

Two good reasons, therefore, given us in the Prayer Book for seeking this help are:

(1) The counsel and advice a wise priest can give which can help so greatly.

(2) The certainty of forgiveness and the joy this brings.

Should you decide to ask your priest to advise you in this way the times when he is available are sometimes made known in church or on the notice board, or you may prefer to seek him in his own house. He will be very happy to help you. Or, if you prefer, you may go to a priest who is a stranger— 'Come to me or to some other discreet and learned minister,' the Prayer Book says.

When you have talked to the priest he may ask you to kneel and use this form of words:

Priest: The Lord be in thy heart and on thy lips that thou mayest faithfully and truly confess thy sins unto him, to the honour and glory of his holy Name.

You now say:

I confess to God Almighty, the Father, the Son and the Holy Ghost and before the whole company of heaven, and to you, my father, that I have sinned exceedingly in thought, word, and deed, through my own grievous fault.
Especially I have sinned in these ways....

(Here name all the sins you can remember. Refer to the list you made at your self-examination.)

For these and all my other sins which I cannot now remember, I am very sorry. I intend to lead a new life. I humbly ask pardon of God, and of you, my father, counsel and absolution.

The priest will give you advice. Then he will pronounce God's forgiveness in the Prayer Book words:

Our Lord Jesus Christ who hath left power to his Church to absolve all sinners who truly repent and believe in him, of his great mercy forgive thee thine offences; and by his authority committed unto me, I absolve thee from all thy sins, in the name of the Father, and of the Son, and of the Holy Ghost. *Amen.*

And he may add:

The Passion of our Lord Jesus Christ and his infinite merits be to thee for remission of sins, for growth in grace, and for the reward of everlasting life.

The Blessing of God Almighty, the Father, the Son, and the Holy Ghost, be with you now and evermore. Amen.

Go in peace. The Lord hath put away thy sins from thee.

Thank God with all your heart for his wonderful generosity and kindness in thus forgiving you.

TWO NEW COMMUNION SERVICES

Jesus gave us the Holy Communion and in it entrusted to us a vital work. One name of this work is the 'Liturgy', which means literally 'the work of the people'. That is one way in which we are to think of the Holy Communion, a work we do for God.

Today, as many times in the past, the Church is up-dating the Liturgy, seeking clearer words and ways in which to express what Jesus does for us in this sacrament of his saving Passion and what we should do for him and for our fellows.

'SERIES TWO' and 'SERIES THREE'

In this up-dating, side by side with the old Communion Service which is retained in language unaltered since Cranmer composed it in English 400 years ago, two new Liturgies have been authorised for experimental use. These are known as Series Two and Series Three. Here they are on the following pages.

It is interesting to see how Series Three (only 'born' in 1973) has grown out of Two. Both are of today. But both are also rooted and grounded in scripture and history.

In them we can truly offer to God 'ourselves, our souls and bodies' and draw strength to serve others. And so worship, work, and service become one through the Liturgy, the work of the people of God.

THE
HOLY COMMUNION
according to the
Series Two LITURGY

NOTES

Sections not preceded by the symbol ▶ and material in [brackets], may be omitted.

The printing of prayers in bold type shows that the People should or may join with the Priest.

The People should say or sing responses printed in bold type.

THE 'SERIES TWO' COMMUNION SERVICE

THE ANTECOMMUNION

INTRODUCTION

1. At the entry of the Ministers a psalm, or portion of a psalm, may be sung, or else a hymn.

2. Then may be said the following prayer.

Almighty God,
unto whom all hearts be open,
all desires known,
and from whom no secrets are hid:
Cleanse the thoughts of our hearts,
by the inspiration of thy Holy Spirit,
that we may perfectly love thee,
and worthily magnify thy holy Name;
through Christ our Lord. Amen.

3. One of the following may be used: either the Ten Commandments, or our Lord's summary of the Law, or the Kyries in English or Greek. The text for these appears in Appendix 1 on pp. 93 and 95.

4. Then may be sung or said,

Glory be to God on high,
and in earth peace, good will towards men.
We praise thee, we bless thee,
we worship thee, we glorify thee,
we give thanks to thee for thy great glory,
O Lord God, heavenly King,
God the Father Almighty.

O Lord, the only-begotten Son, Jesu Christ:
O Lord God, Lamb of God, Son of the Father,
that takest away the sins of the world,
have mercy upon us.
Thou that takest away the sins of the world,
receive our prayer.
Thou that sittest at the right hand of
God the Father, have mercy upon us.

For thou only art Holy;
thou only art the Lord;
thou only, O Christ, with the Holy Ghost,
art the Most High, in the glory of God the Father.
Amen.

▶ 5. Then shall the Priest read the Collect of the Day,
first saying,

> The Lord be with you;
> **And with thy spirit.**
> Let us pray.

THE MINISTRY OF THE WORD

6. A lesson from the Old Testament may then be read.

7. A psalm, or portion of a psalm, may then be sung or
said, or else a canticle, or a hymn.

▶ 8. A lesson from the Old or New Testament shall then
be read.

9. A psalm, or portion of a psalm, may then be sung
or said, or else a canticle, or a hymn.

▶ *10. A lesson from the Gospels shall then be read; and when the Gospel is announced, the People shall answer,*

Glory be to thee, O Lord.

▶ *11. At the end of the Gospel the People shall answer,*

Praise be to thee, O Christ.

12. The sermon shall be preached after the Gospel.

▶ *13. On Sundays and other holy days the Creed shall then be sung or said.*

I believe in one God the Father Almighty,
maker of heaven and earth,
and of all things visible and invisible:

And in one Lord Jesus Christ,
the only-begotten Son of God,
begotten of his Father before all worlds,
God of God, Light of Light, very God of very God,
begotten, not made,
being of one substance with the Father,
by whom all things were made:

who for us men, and for our salvation
came down from heaven,
and was incarnate by the Holy Ghost of the
Virgin Mary, and was made man,
and was crucified also for us under Pontius Pilate.
He suffered and was buried,
and the third day he rose again
according to the scriptures,

and ascended into heaven,
and sitteth on the right hand of the Father.
And he shall come again with glory
to judge both the quick and the dead:
whose kingdom shall have no end.

And I believe in the Holy Ghost,
the Lord, the Giver of life,
who proceedeth from the Father and the Son,
who with the Father and the Son together
is worshipped and glorified,
who spake by the prophets.

And I believe one holy catholic and apostolic
Church.
I acknowledge one Baptism for the remission of
sins.
And I look for the Resurrection of the dead,
and the Life of the world to come. Amen.

INTERCESSION

▶ 14. *The prayers of the Church shall then be offered
by the Priest or by one of the other Ministers.*

Let us pray for the whole Church of God in Christ
Jesus, and for all men according to their needs.

Almighty God, who hast promised to hear the prayers
of those who ask in faith:

*Here he may pray for the Church throughout the
world, and especially for the diocese and its Bishop;
for any particular need of the Church; and a short
period of silence may be kept; after which he may say,*

Lord, in thy mercy
Hear our prayer.

Grant that we who confess thy Name may be united in thy truth, live together in thy love, and show forth thy glory in the world.

Here he may pray for the nations of the world, and especially for this kingdom and Elizabeth its Queen; for all men in their various callings; and again a short period of silence may be kept; after which he may say,

Lord, in thy mercy

Hear our prayer.

Direct this nation and all the nations in the ways of justice and of peace, that we may honour all men, and seek the common good.

Here he may pray for the sick, the poor, and for those in trouble; for the needs of particular persons; and again a short period of silence may be kept; after which he may say,

Lord, in thy mercy

Hear our prayer.

Save and comfort those who suffer, that they may hold to thee through good and ill, and trust in thy unfailing love.

Here he may commemorate the departed: he may commend them by name; and again a short period of silence may be kept; after which he may say,

Lord, in thy mercy

Hear our prayer.

Hear us as we remember those who have died in faith, and grant us with them a share in thy eternal kingdom.

At the end of the prayers he shall say,

Grant these our prayers, O merciful Father, for the sake of thy Son, our Saviour Jesus Christ. **Amen.**

15. The prayers of the Church may be said as one continuous prayer.

16. Banns of Marriage and other notices may then be published, if they have not been published before the service; a hymn may be sung, and the gifts of the People collected; and if there be no Communion THE GRACE OF OUR LORD JESUS CHRIST, etc., may be said.

THE COMMUNION

THE PREPARATION OF THE PEOPLE

▶ 17. Then shall the Priest begin the Communion, saying,

Seeing we have a great high priest who has passed into the heavens, Jesus the Son of God, let us draw near with a true heart, in full assurance of faith, and make our confession to our heavenly Father.

▶ 18. The Minister and People shall then make the following Confession.

Almighty God, our heavenly Father,
we have sinned against thee,
through our own fault,
in thought, and word, and deed,
and in what we have left undone.

**For thy Son our Lord Jesus Christ's sake,
forgive us all that is past;
and grant that we may serve thee
in newness of life,
to the glory of thy Name. Amen.**

19. The Priest shall then say the following Absolution.

Almighty God have mercy upon you, pardon and deliver you from all your sins, confirm and strengthen you in all goodness, and keep you in life eternal; through Jesus Christ our Lord. **Amen.**

20. Here may be said these comfortable words by the Priest, or by one of the other Ministers.

Hear what comfortable words our Saviour Christ
says to all who truly turn to him.

Come unto me, all that travail and are heavy laden, and I will refresh you.

So God loved the world, that he gave his only-begotten Son, to the end that all that believe in him should not perish, but have everlasting life.

Hear also what Saint Paul says.

This is a true saying, and worthy of all men to be received, that Christ Jesus came into the world to save sinners.

Hear also what Saint John says.

If any man sin, we have an advocate with the Father, Jesus Christ the righteous; and he is the propitiation for our sins.

21. Then may be said by the Priest alone, or by Priest and People together, the following prayer.

We do not presume to come to this thy table,
O merciful Lord,
trusting in our own righteousness,
but in thy manifold and great mercies.
We are not worthy so much as to gather up
the crumbs under thy table.
But thou art the same Lord,
whose nature it is always to have mercy.
Grant us therefore, gracious Lord,
so to eat the Flesh of thy dear Son Jesus Christ,
and to drink his Blood,
that we may evermore dwell in him, and he in us.
Amen.

22. *Then the Priest may say,*
We are the Body of Christ. By one Spirit we were all
baptized into one Body. Endeavour to keep the unity
of the Spirit in the bond of peace.

> The peace of the Lord be always with you;
> **And with thy spirit.**

THE PREPARATION OF THE BREAD AND WINE

▶ 23. *Then shall bread and wine be placed in order
upon the Holy Table; and the gifts of the People may
be collected and presented at the same time. Mean-
while, a hymn may be sung.*

THE THANKSGIVING

▶ 24. *Then shall the Priest at once begin the Prayer of
Consecration, saying,*
> The Lord be with you;

And with thy spirit.

Lift up your hearts;

We lift them up unto the Lord.

Let us give thanks unto the Lord our God;

It is meet and right so to do.

It is very meet, right, and our bounden duty, that we should at all times, and in all places, give thanks unto thee, O Lord, holy Father, almighty, everlasting God, through Jesus Christ, thine only Son, our Lord;

Because through him thou hast created all things from the beginning, and fashioned us men in thine own image;

Through him thou didst redeem us from the slavery of sin, giving him to be born as man, to die upon the cross, and to rise again for us;

During Christmastide insert here,

For by the operation of the Holy Spirit he was made man of the Virgin Mary his mother; and that without spot of sin, to make us clean from all sin;

During Passiontide insert here,

For being found in fashion as a man he humbled himself, and became obedient unto death, even the death of the cross; wherefore thou hast raised him from the dead, and given him the Name that is above every name;

During Eastertide insert here,

For he is the true Paschal Lamb which was offered for us, and has taken away the sin of the world; who by his death has destroyed death, and by his rising to life again has restored to us everlasting life;

Through him thou hast made us a people for thine own possession, exalting him to thy right hand on high, and sending forth through him thy holy and life-giving Spirit;

From Ascension Day to the Saturday after Pentecost insert here,

For by the gift of that same Spirit thou hast empowered thy people to preach the Gospel among the nations, and to serve thee acceptably as a royal priesthood;

Through him therefore, with angels and archangels, and with all the company of heaven, we laud and magnify thy glorious Name, evermore praising thee, and saying,

Holy, Holy, Holy, Lord God of Hosts,
Heaven and earth are full of thy glory,
Glory be to thee, O Lord most high.

Hear us, O Father, through Christ thy Son our Lord; through him accept our sacrifice of praise; and grant that these gifts of bread and wine may be unto us his Body and Blood;

Who in the same night that he was betrayed[1] took bread; and, when he had given thanks to thee, he broke it, and gave it to his disciples, saying, Take, eat; this is my Body which is given for you; Do this in remembrance of me. Likewise after supper he[2] took the cup; and, when he had given thanks to thee, he gave it to them, saying, Drink ye all of this; for this is my Blood of the new covenant, which is shed for you and for many for the remission of sins; Do this, as oft as ye shall drink it, in remembrance of me.

1 Here the Priest is to take the bread into his hands.

2 Here he is to take the cup into his hands.

Wherefore, O Lord, with this bread and this cup we make the memorial of his saving passion, his resurrection from the dead, and his glorious ascension into heaven, and we look for the coming of his kingdom. We pray thee to accept this our duty and service, and grant that we may so eat and drink these holy things in the presence of thy divine majesty, that we may be filled with thy grace and heavenly blessing;

Through the same Christ our Lord, by whom, and with whom, and in whom, in the unity of the Holy

Spirit, all honour and glory be unto thee, O Father Almighty, from the whole company of earth and heaven, throughout all ages, world without end.

▶ 25. *And all the People shall say,*

Amen.

▶ 26. *This anthem may be sung or said.*

Blessed is he that cometh in the name of the Lord. Hosanna in the highest.

THE BREAKING OF THE BREAD

▶ 27. *Then shall the consecrated bread be broken into pieces; and first may be said,*

**The cup of blessing which we bless,
is it not a sharing of the Blood of Christ?
The bread which we break,
is it not a sharing of the Body of Christ?
We being many are one bread, one Body,
for we all partake of the one bread.**

28. *While the consecrated bread is being broken, the following anthem may be sung.*

**O Lamb of God, that takest away the sins of the world, have mercy upon us.
O Lamb of God, that takest away the sins of the world, have mercy upon us.
O Lamb of God, that takest away the sins of the world, grant us thy peace.**

THE SHARING OF THE BREAD AND WINE

29. Then shall the Priest and People together say the
Lord's Prayer, the Priest first saying,

Let us pray.

As our Saviour Christ has commanded and taught us,
we are bold to say,

**Our Father, who art in heaven,
hallowed be thy name;
thy kingdom come;
thy will be done;
on earth as it is in heaven.
Give us this day our daily bread.
And forgive us our trespasses,
as we forgive those who trespass against us.
And lead us not into temptation;
but deliver us from evil. Amen.**

▶ 30. Then shall the Priest and the other Ministers themselves receive the consecrated bread and wine, and shall deliver them to the People; and first the Priest may say,

Draw near with faith: receive the Body of our Lord Jesus Christ, which was given for you, and his Blood, which was shed for you; and feed on him in your heart by faith with thanksgiving.

▶ 31. He who delivers the consecrated bread and wine shall say to each one who receives,

The Body of Christ

and

The Blood of Christ

and he who receives shall reply,

Amen.

32. Or else he who delivers the consecrated bread and wine shall say,

The Body of our Lord Jesus Christ, which was given for you, preserve your body and soul to everlasting life.

Take and eat this in remembrance that Christ died for you, and feed on him in your heart by faith with thanksgiving.

and

The Blood of our Lord Jesus Christ, which was shed for you, preserve your body and soul to everlasting life.

Drink this in remembrance that Christ's Blood was shed for you, and be thankful.

33. While the People are receiving, hymns and anthems may be sung.

APPENDIX 1

THE TEN COMMANDMENTS

God spake these words and said:
I am the Lord thy God; thou shalt have none other gods but me.

Lord, have mercy upon us, and incline our hearts to keep this law.

Thou shalt not make to thyself any graven image, nor the likeness of anything that is in heaven above, or in the earth beneath, or in the water under the earth. Thou shalt not bow down to them, nor worship them.

Lord, have mercy upon us, and incline our hearts to keep this law.

Thou shalt not take the Name of the Lord thy God in vain.

Lord, have mercy upon us, and incline our hearts to keep this law.

Remember that thou keep holy the Sabbath day. Six days shalt thou labour, and do all that thou hast to do; but the seventh day is the Sabbath of the Lord thy God.

Lord, have mercy upon us, and incline our hearts to keep this law.

Honour thy father and thy mother.

Lord, have mercy upon us, and incline our hearts to keep this law.

Thou shalt do no murder.

Lord, have mercy upon us, and incline our hearts to keep this law.

Thou shalt not commit adultery.

Lord, have mercy upon us, and incline our hearts to keep this law.

Thou shalt not steal.

Lord, have mercy upon us, and incline our hearts to keep this law.

Thou shalt not bear false witness.

Lord, have mercy upon us, and incline our hearts to keep this law.

Thou shalt not covet.

Lord, have mercy upon us, and write all these thy laws in our hearts, we beseech thee.

OUR LORD'S SUMMARY OF THE LAW

Our Lord Jesus Christ said: Hear O Israel, The Lord our God is one Lord; and thou shalt love the Lord thy God with all thy heart, and with all thy soul, and with all thy mind, and with all thy strength. This is the first commandment. And the second is like, namely this: Thou shalt love thy neighbour as thyself. There is none other commandment greater than these. On these two commandments hang all the law and the prophets.

Lord, have mercy upon us, and write both these thy laws in our hearts, we beseech thee.

THE KYRIES

Lord, have mercy.	(Kyrie eleison.)
Lord, have mercy.	**Kyrie eleison.**
Lord, have mercy.	Kyrie eleison.
Christ, have mercy.	**Christe eleison.**
Christ, have mercy.	Christe eleison.
Christ, have mercy.	**Christe eleison.**
Lord, have mercy.	Kyrie eleison.
Lord, have mercy.	**Kyrie eleison.**
Lord, have mercy.	(Kyrie eleison.)

THE
HOLY COMMUNION
according to the
Series Three LITURGY

NOTES

Sections preceded by the symbol ▶ are mandatory.
Sections not preceded by this symbol are optional.

THE WORD AND THE PRAYERS

THE PREPARATION

2 *At the entry of the ministers a sentence may be used;*
   and a hymn, a canticle, or a psalm may be sung.

3 *The minister may say*

> The Lord be with you.
> **And also with you.**

4 *The following prayer may be said.*

> **Almighty God,**
> **to whom all hearts are open,**
> **all desires known,**
> **and from whom no secrets are hid:**
> **cleanse the thoughts of our hearts**
> **by the inspiration of your Holy Spirit,**
> **that we may perfectly love you,**
> **and worthily magnify your holy Name;**
> **through Christ our Lord. Amen.**

5 *The Kyries may be said.*

> Lord, have mercy.
> **Lord, have mercy.**
> Lord, have mercy.
>
> **Christ, have mercy.**
> Christ, have mercy.
> **Christ, have mercy.**
>
> Lord, have mercy.
> **Lord, have mercy.**
> Lord, have mercy.

Or the canticle Gloria in Excelsis may be said.

Glory to God in the highest,
and peace to his people on earth.

Lord God, heavenly King,
almighty God and Father,
we worship you, we give you thanks,
we praise you for your glory.

Lord Jesus Christ, only Son of the
    Father,
Lord God, Lamb of God,
you take away the sin of the world:
have mercy on us;
you are seated at the the right hand
    of the Father:
receive our prayer.

For you alone are the Holy One,
you alone are the Lord,
you alone are the Most High,
Jesus Christ with the Holy Spirit,
in the glory of God the Father. Amen.

▶ 6 *The collect of the day.*

THE MINISTRY OF THE WORD

▶ 7 SIT
The Old Testament lesson. At the end there may be said

Reader   This is the word of the Lord.
Thanks be to God.

Silence may be kept.

8 *A psalm may be said.*

▶ 9 *The Epistle. At the end there may be said*

Reader   This is the word of the Lord.
Thanks be to God.

Silence may be kept.

10 *A canticle, a hymn, or a psalm may be sung.*

11 STAND
The Gospel. When it is announced

Glory to Christ our Saviour.

At the end the reader says

This is the Gospel of Christ.

Praise to Christ our Lord.

Silence may be kept.

12 SIT
The sermon.
At the end silence may be kept.

▶ 13 STAND
The Nicene Creed is said, at least on Sundays and
greater Holy Days.

We believe in one God,
the Father, the Almighty,
maker of heaven and earth,
of all that is seen and unseen.

We believe in one Lord, Jesus Christ,
the only Son of God,
eternally begotten of the Father.
God from God, Light from Light,
true God from true God,
begotten, not made,
one in Being with the Father.
Through him all things were made.
For us men and for our salvation
he came down from heaven;
by the power of the Holy Spirit
he was born of the Virgin Mary,
    and became man.
For our sake he was crucified
    under Pontius Pilate;
he suffered, died, and was buried.
On the third day he rose again
in fulfilment of the Scriptures;
he ascended into heaven
and is seated at the right hand
    of the Father.
He will come again in glory
to judge the living and the dead,
and his kingdom will have no end.
We believe in the Holy Spirit, the
    Lord, the giver of life.
who proceeds from the Father
    and the Son.

With the Father and the Son he is
    worshipped and glorified.
He has spoken through the Prophets.
We believe in one holy catholic
    and apostolic Church.
We acknowledge one baptism
    for the forgiveness of sins.
We look for the resurrection of the
dead, and the life of the world to come.
                    Amen.

THE PRAYERS

4 *Banns of marriage and other notices may be
published; the offerings of the people may be
collected; and a hymn may be sung.*

5 *Intercessions and thanksgivings are offered
by the president or by some other person.
These may be introduced by biddings.
It is not necessary to include specific subjects
in any section of the following prayer.
The set passages may also follow one another as
a continuous whole, without versicles and
responses.*

   Minister   Let us pray for the Church and for the
                 world; and let us thank God for his
                 goodness.
                 Almighty God, our heavenly Father,
                 who promised through your Son
                 Jesus Christ to hear us when we
                 pray in faith:

We give thanks for/we pray for
the Church throughout the world . . .
our own Church, our diocese and bishop . .
any particular work of the Church . . .

Silence may be kept.

Strengthen your Church to carry
forward the work of Christ; that we and
all who confess your Name may unite
in your truth, live together in your love,
and reveal your glory in the world.

Lord, in your mercy

Hear our prayer.

We give thanks for/we pray for
the nations of the world . . .
our own nation . . .
all men in their various callings . . .

Silence may be kept.

Give wisdom to all in authority,
especially Elizabeth our Queen; direct
this nation and all nations in the ways
of justice and of peace; that men may
honour one another, and seek the
common good.

Lord, in your mercy

Hear our prayer.

We give thanks for/we pray for
the local community . . .
our families and friends . . .
particular persons . . .

Silence may be kept.

Give grace to us, our families and friends, and to all our neighbours in Christ; that we may serve him in one another, and love as he loves us.

Lord, in your mercy

Hear our prayer.

We pray for
the sick and the suffering . . .
those who mourn . . .
those without faith . . .

We give thanks and pray for
all who serve and relieve them . . .

Silence may be kept.

Comfort and heal all those who suffer
in body, mind, or spirit; give them
courage and hope in their troubles; and
bring them the joy of your salvation.

Lord, in your mercy

Hear our prayer.

We commemorate
the departed, especially . . .

Silence may be kept.

We commend all men to your unfailing
love, that in them your will may be
fulfilled; and we rejoice at the faithful
witness of your saints in every age,
praying that we may share with them in
your eternal kingdom.

Lord, in your mercy

**Accept these prayers
for the sake of your Son,
our Saviour Jesus Christ. Amen.**

16 The minister may say the Commandments (pp.118-
120) and silence may be kept after the responses;
or the Summary of the Law may be said (p. 120).

▶ 17 Minister   God so loved the world that he gave his
only Son, Jesus Christ, to save us from
our sins, to be our advocate in heaven,
and to bring us to eternal life.

Let us therefore confess our sins, in
penitence and faith, firmly resolved to
keep God's commandments and to live
in love and peace with all men.

Or he says one or more of these sentences:

Hear the words of comfort our Saviour
Christ says to all who truly turn to him.

Come to me, all who labour and are
heavy-laden, and I will give you rest.

God so loved the world that he gave his
only Son, that whoever believes in him
should not perish but have eternal life.

Hear what St Paul says.

This saying is true and worthy of full
acceptance, that Christ Jesus
came into the world to save sinners.

Hear what St John says.

If anyone does sin, we have an
advocate with the Father, Jesus Christ
the righteous; and he is the expiation
of our sins.

After which he says:

Let us therefore confess our sins, in
penitence and faith, firmly resolved
to keep God's commandments and
to live in love and peace with all men.

Silence may be kept.

Almighty God, our heavenly Father,
we have sinned against you and
   against our fellow men,
in thought and word and deed,
in the evil we have done
and in the good we have not done,
through ignorance, through weakness,
through our own deliberate fault.
We are truly sorry and repent
   of all our sins.
For the sake of your Son, Jesus Christ,
   who died for us,
forgive us all that is past;
and grant that we may serve you
   in newness of life
to the glory of your Name. Amen.

▶ 19 President Almighty God, who forgives all who
truly repent, have mercy upon you,
pardon and deliver you from all your
sins, confirm and strengthen you in all
goodness, and keep you in life eternal;
through Jesus Christ our Lord.

Amen.

20 *All may say* We do not presume to
come to this your table, merciful Lord,
trusting in our own righteousness,
but in your manifold and great mercies.
We are not worthy
so much as to gather up the crumbs
   under your table.

But you are the same Lord
whose nature is always to have mercy.
Grant us therefore gracious Lord,
so to eat the flesh of your dear Son
    Jesus Christ,
and to drink his blood,
that we may evermore dwell in him,
and he in us. Amen.

THE COMMUNION

THE PEACE

▶ 21 *STAND*

    President   We are the Body of Christ.
In the one Spirit we were all baptized
into one body. Let us then pursue all
that makes for peace and builds up our
common life.

▶ 22 *The president gives the Peace to the congregation, saying:*

The peace of the Lord be always
with you.

And also with you.

THE TAKING OF THE BREAD AND WINE

  23 *A hymn may be sung, and the offerings of the people may be collected and presented.*

▶ 24 *The bread and wine are brought to the holy table, and this sentence may be used:*

**Yours, Lord, is the greatness, the
power, the glory, the splendour and
the majesty; for everything in heaven
and on earth is yours.
All things come from you, and of your
own do we give you.**

▶ 25 *The president takes the bread and wine.*

THE THANKSGIVING

▶ *26 The president says,*

> The Lord is here.
> **His Spirit is with us.**

President Lift up your hearts.
> **We lift them to the Lord.**

President Let us give thanks to the Lord our God.
> **It is right to give him thanks and praise.**

▶ *27 President* It is not only right, it is our duty and our
joy, at all times and in all places, to give
you thanks and praise, holy Father,
heavenly King, almighty and eternal
God, through Jesus Christ, your only
Son, our Lord;

For he is your living Word; through him
you have created all things from the
beginning, and formed us in your own
image;

Through him you have freed us from
the slavery of sin, giving him to be born
as man, to die upon the cross, and
to rise again for us;

Through him you have made us a people
for your own possession, exalting him
to your right hand on high, and sending
upon us your holy and life-giving Spirit.

And now we give you thanks, because...

Here a seasonal sentence may be said.

29

Therefore with angels and archangels,
and with all the company of heaven, we
proclaim your great and glorious Name,
for ever praising you and saying:

Holy, holy, holy Lord,
God of power and might,
Heaven and earth are full of your glory.
Hosanna in the highest.

President

Accept our praises, heavenly Father,
through your Son, our Saviour Jesus
Christ; and as we follow his example
and obey his command, grant that by
the power of your Spirit these gifts
of bread and wine may be to us his body
and his blood;

For in the same night that he was
betrayed, he took bread; and after giving
you thanks, he broke it, gave it to his
disciples, and said, 'Take, eat; this is my
body which is given for you. Do this in
remembrance of me.' Again, after
supper he took the cup; he gave you
thanks, and gave it to them, saying,
'Drink this, all of you; for this is my
blood of the new Covenant, which
is shed for you and for many, for the
forgiveness of sins. Do this, as often as
you drink it, in remembrance of me.'

Christ has died:
Christ is risen:
Christ will come again.

President Therefore, heavenly Father, with this
bread and this cup we do this in
remembrance of him: we celebrate and
proclaim his perfect sacrifice made
once for all upon the cross, his
resurrection from the dead, and his
ascension into heaven; and we look for
his coming in glory. Accept through
him, our great high priest, this our
sacrifice of thanks and praise; and as
we eat and drink these holy gifts in the
presence of your divine majesty, renew
us by your Spirit, inspire us with your
love, and unite us in the body of your
Son, Jesus Christ our Lord.

With him, and in him, and through him,
by the power of the Holy Spirit, with
all who stand before you in earth and
heaven, we worship you, Father
Almighty, in songs of everlasting praise:

Blessing and honour and glory and
power be yours for ever and ever.
                                    Amen.

Silence may be kept.

THE BREAKING OF THE BREAD

▶ 30 *The president breaks the consecrated bread, saying:*

> We break this bread
> to share in the body of Christ.
>
> **Though we are many, we are one body,
> because we all share in one bread.**

THE GIVING OF THE BREAD AND THE CUP

▶ 31 President   As our Saviour has taught us,
      so we pray:

> **Our Father in heaven,
> hallowed be your Name,
> your kingdom come,
> your will be done,
> on earth as in heaven.
> Give us today our daily bread.
> Forgive us our sins
> as we forgive those who sin against us**
> **Do not bring us to the time of trial
> but deliver us from evil.**
>
> **For the kingdom, the power, and
>   the glory are yours
> now and for ever. Amen.**

▶ 32 President   Draw near with faith. Receive the body
      of our Lord Jesus Christ which he gave
      for you, and his blood which he shed
      for you. Remember that he died for you,
      and feed on him in your hearts by faith
      with thanksgiving.

33 The president and the other communicants receive the holy communion.

At the administration the ministers say to each communicant,

> The Body of Christ keep you
> in eternal life.

> The Blood of Christ keep you
> in eternal life.

The communicant replies each time,

> **Amen.**

and then receives.

34 During the Communion these and other hymns and anthems may be sung:

> **Blessed is he who comes in the name
> of the Lord. Hosanna in the highest.**

> **Jesus, Lamb of God: have mercy on us.
> Jesus, bearer of our sins: have mercy
> on us.
> Jesus, redeemer of the world: give us
> your peace.**

36 Any consecrated bread and wine which is not required for purposes of communion is consumed at the end of the administration, or after the service.

AFTER COMMUNION

37 *A seasonal sentence may be said.*

Silence may be kept.

▶ 38 *Either or both of the following prayers are said.*

▶ 39 President Father of all, we give you thanks and
praise, that when we were still far off
you met us in your Son and brought us
home. Dying and living, he declared
your love, gave us grace, and opened
the gate of glory. May we who share
Christ's body live his risen life; we who
drink his cup bring life to others; we
whom the Spirit lights give light to the
world. Keep us in this hope that we
have grasped; so we and all your
children shall be free, and the whole
earth live to praise your Name;
through Christ our Lord.
Amen.

▶ 40 **Almighty God,**
we thank you for feeding us
with the body and blood of your Son
Jesus Christ.
Through him we offer you
our souls and bodies
to be a living sacrifice.
Send us out
in the power of your Spirit
to live and work
to your praise and glory. Amen.

41 *A hymn or canticle may be sung.*

42 *The president may say this or the appropriate seasonal blessing.*

> The peace of God, which passes all understanding, keep your hearts and minds in the knowledge and love of God, and of his Son Jesus Christ our Lord; And the blessing of God Almighty, the Father, the Son, and the Holy Spirit, be among you, and remain with you always. **Amen.**

43 President   Go in peace and serve the Lord.

In the name of Christ. Amen.

44 *The Ministers and people depart.*

APPENDIX: THE COMMANDMENTS

Minister   Our Lord Jesus Christ said, If you love
me, keep my commandments: happy
are those who hear the word of God
and keep it. Hear then these commandments which God has given to
his people, and take them to heart.
I am the Lord your God: you shall
have no other gods but me.
You shall love the Lord your God with
all your heart, with all your soul, with
all your mind, and with all your strength.

Amen. Lord, have mercy.

Minister   You shall not make for yourself any idol.
God is spirit, and those who worship
him must worship in spirit and in truth.

Amen. Lord, have mercy.

Minister   You shall not dishonour the name of
the Lord your God.
You shall worship him with reverence
and awe.

Amen. Lord, have mercy.

Minister   Remember the Lord's day and keep it
holy.
Christ is risen from the dead; set
your minds on things that are above,
not on things that are on the earth.

Amen. Lord, have mercy.

Minister	Honour your father and mother. Live as servants of God: honour all men; love the brotherhood.

Amen. Lord, have mercy.

Minister	You shall not commit murder. Do not nurse anger against your brother; overcome evil with good.

Amen. Lord, have mercy.

Minister	You shall not commit adultery. Know that your body is a temple of the Holy Spirit.

Amen. Lord, have mercy.

Minister   You shall not steal.
You shall work honestly and
give to those in need.

Amen. Lord, have mercy.

Minister   You shall not be a false witness.
Let everyone speak the truth.

Amen. Lord, have mercy.

Minister   You shall not covet anything which
belongs to your neighbour.
Remember the words of the Lord
Jesus: It is more blessed to give than
to receive. Love your neighbour as
yourself, for love is the fulfilling of
the law.

Amen. Lord, have mercy.

THE SUMMARY OF THE LAW

Minister   Our Lord Jesus Christ said: The Lord
our God is the only Lord. You shall
love the Lord your God with all your
heart, with all your soul, with all your
mind, and with all your strength. This
is the first commandment. The second
is this: Love your neighbour as
yourself. There is no other commandment greater than these.

Amen. Lord, have mercy.

PRIVATE THANKSGIVINGS AND PRAYERS

to be said in Church and at home

AFTER HOLY COMMUNION

We have offered our joyful sacrifice of praise and thanksgiving. We have pleaded our Lord's 'one, true, pure, immortal sacrifice' for our salvation. We have received the 'means of grace', our chief 'hope of glory'. Let us thank God for our 'redemption . . . by our Lord Jesus Christ'.

Almighty God, Father of all mercies, We thine unworthy servants do give thee most humble and hearty thanks for all thy goodness and loving kindness to us, and to all men.

We bless thee for our creation, preservation, and all the blessings of this life; but above all, for thine inestimable love in the redemption of the world by our Lord Jesus Christ; For the means of grace, and for the hope of glory.

And, we beseech thee, give us that due sense of all thy mercies, that our hearts may be unfeignedly thankful, and that we shew forth thy praise, not only with our lips, but in our lives; by giving up ourselves to thy service, and by walking before thee in holiness and righteousness all our days; through Jesus Christ our Lord, to whom with thee and the Holy Ghost be all honour and glory, world without end. Amen.

Pray for grace to live a Christian life and a useful one in the strength of the Blessed Sacrament.

Strengthen for service, Lord, the hands
 That holy things have taken;
Let ears that now have heard thy songs
 To clamour never waken.

Lord, may the tongues which 'Holy' sang
 Keep free from all deceiving;
The eyes which saw thy love be bright,
 Thy blessed hope perceiving.

The feet that tread thy holy courts
 From light do thou not banish;
The bodies by thy Body fed
 With thy new life replenish.

Epistle, Gospel, Sermon, have spoken of Christ's way. Think again of their message. Pray for grace to walk in that way. You may like to make the Sign of the Cross as you say slowly and prayerfully:

May the grace of our Lord Jesus Christ, and the love of God, and the fellowship of the Holy Spirit, be with me now and always.   Amen.

RULE OF LIFE:

Prayer

Bible

Worship in Church

Communion

Work

Study

Giving

FAVOURITE TEXTS AND PRAYERS

FAVOURITE TEXTS AND PRAYERS

FAVOURITE TEXTS AND PRAYERS